ANIMAL ADVENTURES

Scribble Sprout

Copyright

No part of this book may be reproduced or transmitted in any form or by any means, electronic or mechanical, including photocopying, recording or any information storage or retrieval system without permission from the copyright holder.

Cover by Scribble Sprout

First edition 2024

To contact the Author, please do so through the website.

Author Website: www.scribblesprout.neuvare.com

Publisher: Neuvare

Publisher website: www.neuvare.com

Table of Contents

Introduction to the Animal Kingdom

Hey little friends! Guess what? Our planet Earth is like a big playground filled with so many amazing animals! They come in all shapes and sizes, and there are more than a million of them!

Let's talk about mammals first. Elephants, whales, bats, mice, rabbits, and even humans are all mammals. They have special things like milk-producing glands and hair that make them unique. There are over 5,400 different kinds of mammals all around the world!

Next up are birds! Birds have feathers and some can fly with their special hollow bones.

Eagles, penguins, ostriches, and hummingbirds are some of the cool birds out there. Did you know there are around 10,000 different bird species? They live in places like the Arctic and deserts.

Now, let's hop over to reptiles. Snakes, lizards, crocodiles, turtles, and their friends have scales and like to live on land. There are over 10,000 kinds of reptiles, and they help control pests and recycle nutrients in the environment.

What about frogs and their buddies? They are called amphibians. Frogs, toads, and salamanders live near water, and they can change from babies to adults in a process called metamorphosis. Amphibians are found all over the world except in Antarctica.

Now, let's dive into the oceans and talk about fish! From huge whale sharks to tiny gobies, there are over 32,000 types of fish. They have different jaw structures and live in oceans, rivers, and lakes. Fish actually make up more than half of all the animals with backbones!

But wait, there's more! Insects, spiders, and other creatures without backbones are called invertebrates. They make up over 95% of all known animals! Insects alone have more than 900,000 different types, like ants, butterflies, and beetles. Wow!

And don't forget about slugs, snails, clams, and octopuses. They're called molluscs, and there are over 200,000 of them. They have soft bodies and some even have shells made of calcium carbonate.

Now, let's talk about tiny water bears, also known as tardigrades. They're super small but super tough! They can survive extreme cold, heat, radiation, and even space. Nature is really amazing!

So, you see, our planet is like a big animal party with so many friends. Each animal has a special role in keeping everything balanced and happy. It's like a big family, and we need to take care of them and their homes. Remember, the more we understand and love our animal friends, the better we can take care of our planet!

Exploring Where Animals Come From

Once upon a time, a long, long time ago, there were no animals on Earth. But then, something amazing happened! Soft-bodied marine creatures like sponges, jellyfish, and worms were the first to appear. They didn't have hard shells or skeletons, and they lived in the oceans, filtering food from the water and crawling along the seafloor.

As time passed, about 540 million years ago, during the Cambrian period, more and more animals started to show up.

Fossils from this time tell us about the ancestors of animals like molluscs, arthropods, echinoderms, and jawless fish. These creatures began to compete and evolve into different shapes and sizes, with some becoming predators that hunted for their food.

Around 400 million years ago, some fish decided to explore the land. They developed legs and rudimentary lungs, becoming the first amphibians. Even though they still needed water to have babies, they made a big leap onto solid ground. This was a huge change that required them to adapt to gravity, different weather, and dry land.

After a while, about 320 million years ago, reptiles evolved from amphibians. They were smart because they started laying eggs with tough membranes, allowing them to live and reproduce on dry land without needing water. With their scaly skin and efficient breathing, reptiles could thrive in many different places, even arid environments.

Then, 230 million years ago, dinosaurs appeared and ruled the land for a very, very long time.

There were plant-eating dinosaurs and meat-eating dinosaurs, and they were the big bosses everywhere on Earth. But, sadly, a big rock from space came crashing down, and it changed everything. The dinosaurs went away, making room for the age of mammals.

Mammals, like monkeys, apes, and humans, started to take over.

Whales, too, went back to the oceans, leaving their land life behind. Birds, on the other hand, descended from dinosaurs and adapted with feathers, hollow bones, and hard-shelled eggs. They spread across the world, making homes in different places.

Insects, like ants and butterflies, also joined the party. They became 75% of all the known animals, living on land, in freshwater, and even in the ocean. Their small bodies and quick life cycles helped them change and evolve really fast.

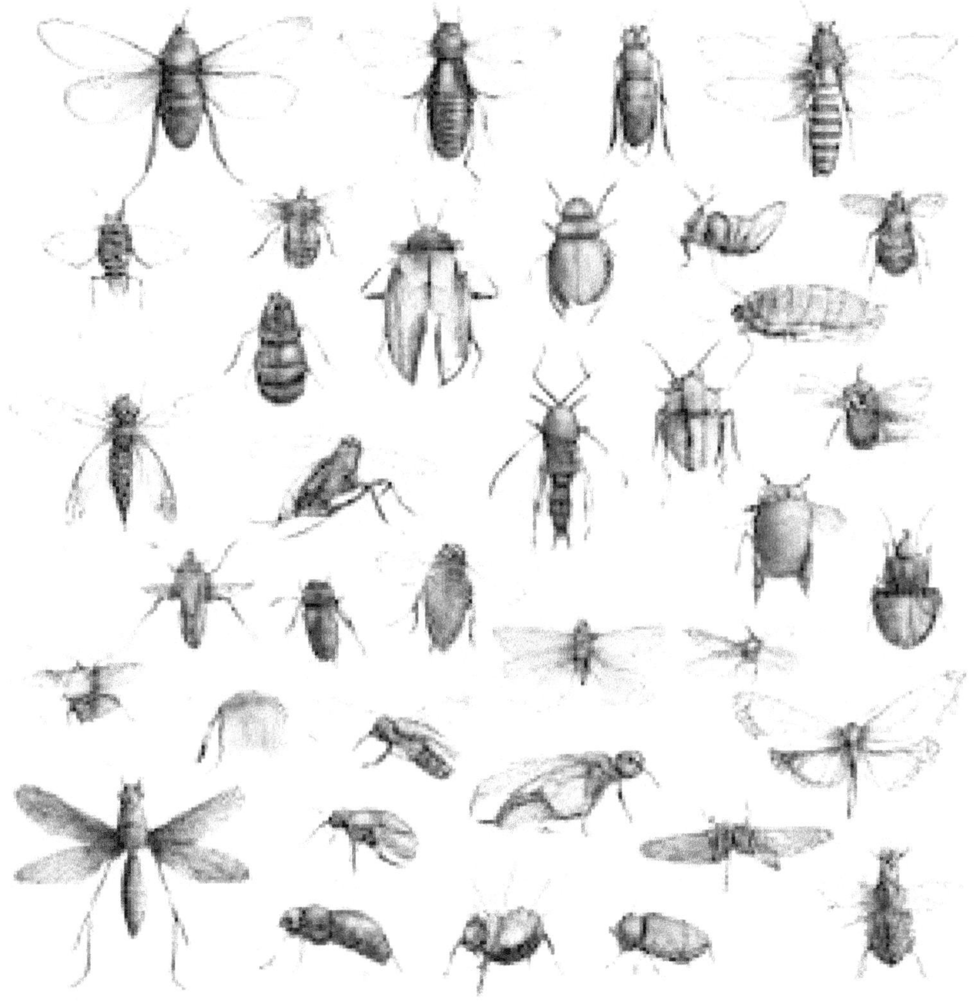

Now, when scientists look at fossils, embryos, and DNA, they can tell the amazing stories of how all these animals came to be. Even though we might not know everything, one thing is for sure — animals are like a big family tree, with each branch telling a different tale. And guess what?

We're all part of this family too! So, let's be kind to our animal friends and remember that we're all in this adventure together, from a long time ago to now!

Animal Groups

Deep in our world, there are lots and lots of different animals. Figuring out who is who can be a big challenge, but some smart scientists had a plan! They use special rules to put animals into groups and give them names.

The first big group is called the "kingdom," and every animal is in the "Animalia" kingdom. This separates animals from things like plants and bacteria. Animals have things in common, like having many cells and not being able to make food from the sun.

Inside the animal kingdom, there are about 35 special groups called "phyla." These groups are like big families that have animals with similar bodies. For example, vertebrates, like us humans, are in the "Chordata" phylum. Other creatures, like spiders and insects, have their own phyla. These groups help us understand the different shapes and sizes of animals.

Next, there's a level called "class," which divides the phyla even more based on special features. Mammals, like dogs and cats, are in the "Mammalia" class. There are other classes for birds, reptiles, and more. It's like a big family with smaller groups inside.

Below the class, there are "orders" that share even more specific things. Families come next, grouping animals together based on how they look and act. For example, lions and tigers belong to the "Carnivora" order, and felines, canines, and ursines are families in that group.

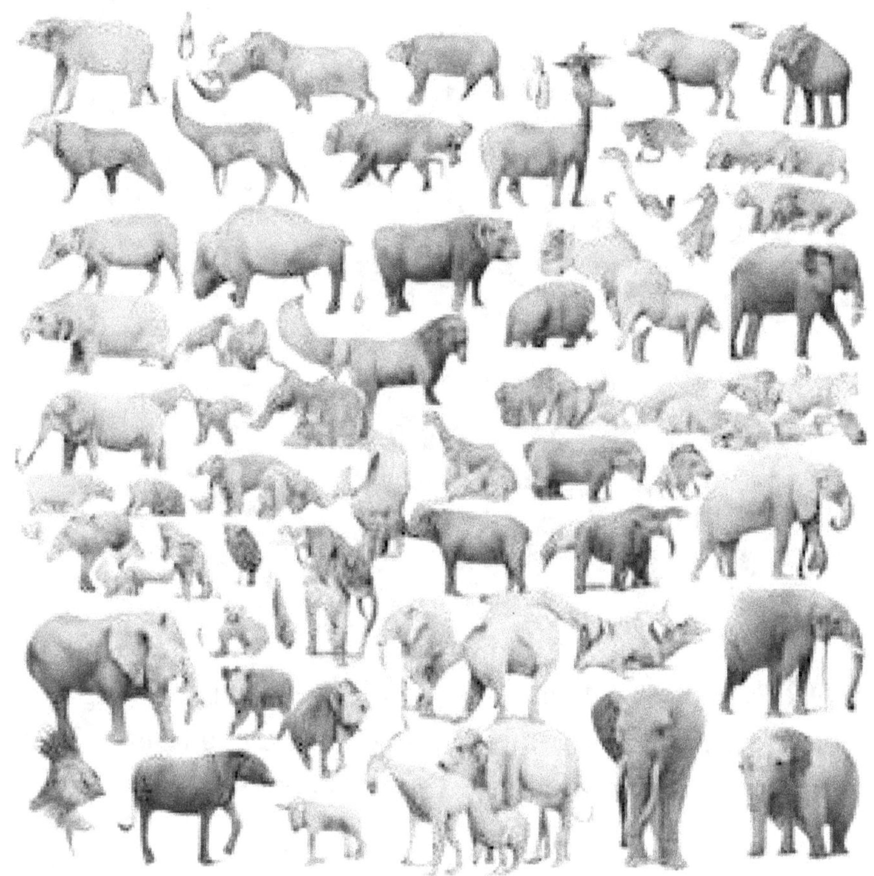

Then comes "genera," which are like super-close families. Animals in the same genus are really similar and usually can't have babies with animals from a different genus. Big cats like lions and tigers are part of the "Panthera" genus.

The smallest group is the "species," which are animals that are very, very similar and can have babies together. Grey wolves and red wolves, even though they look alike, belong to different species.

But here's the fun part – nature doesn't always follow the rules perfectly! Some animals, like the duck-billed platypus, don't fit neatly into one category. And sometimes, animals mix and match, creating hybrids.

Even though these rules help us understand animals better, we have to remember that they're like a guide, not a strict rulebook. Scientists keep learning more, and they might even add more groups to make the system even better!

So, by using this special system called taxonomy, we can figure out where each animal fits in the big family of life. It's like a puzzle, and every piece, big or small, plays a special role in our amazing world!

Animal Minds

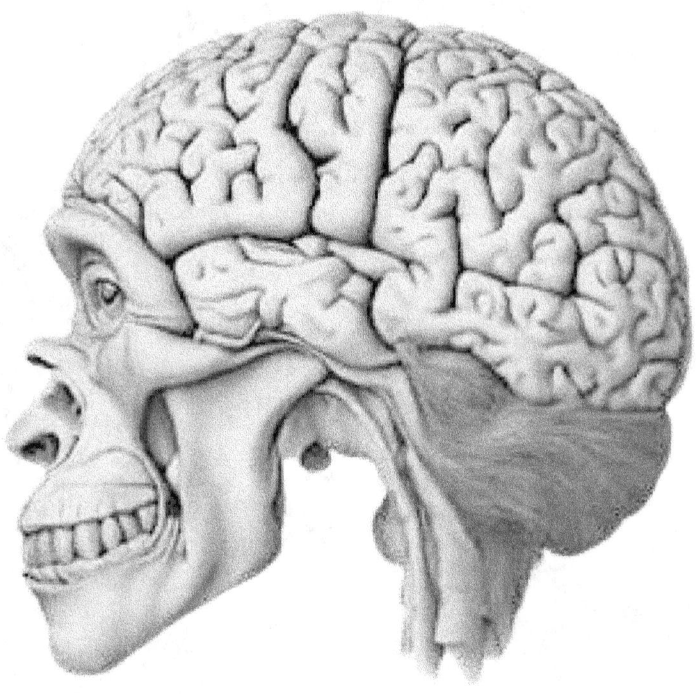

Hey there, little friends! Isn't it super cool to learn about our animal buddies and how smart they are? Animals have amazing brains, just like us, and they can do some really awesome things!

Let's talk about memory first. Did you know that some animals can remember things from a really, really long time ago? Like, African grey parrots, they can remember words they learned many years ago, and dogs can remember the names of lots and lots of toys! Humans have super good memories, but animals are pretty impressive ones too!

Now, let's chat about learning and problem-solving. Crows are like little inventors – they use tools they find to get their yummy food! And gorillas can understand over a thousand signs in sign language – that's a lot! Even octopuses are like undersea engineers, opening jars to get to their snacks. And guess what? Clever crows in New Caledonia use three-part tools to catch their dinner – that's some serious brainpower!

Animals can also be like superheroes in the mirror test. Some animals, like chimpanzees and orcas, can recognise themselves in a mirror! It's like they know they are special and unique, just like you! And did you know that prairie vole have their own language? They can tell each other about humans, describing if someone is tall or short, heavy or thin – it's like having their own secret code!

Oh, and animals are also great at being social. Elephants have strong family bonds and even have special rituals for when someone is feeling sad. Great apes, like gorillas and chimpanzees, learn from each other and share cool ideas. And guess what? Some animals, like ravens, know how to play and have fun – just like us!

Even though humans are super good at some things, animals have their own amazing abilities. We're all connected in a big, awesome family with animals. We're still learning about their super cool minds, and it's like a big adventure discovering all the wonderful things they can do. So, let's be friends with our animal pals and keep exploring together!

Animal Emotions

Animals are not just smart, they also have feelings, just like us! Let's explore how animals show their emotions in special ways.

When an animal loses a friend, like an elephant losing another elephant, they feel really sad. Elephants might stay close to their friend's body or even cover them with leaves and dirt. Dolphins are super caring too—they stay with their sick friends, even after they pass away. And just like us, chimpanzees can feel really sad when a family member is gone.

Animals also know how to be kind. Rats won't eat food if it hurts their rat friends. Monkeys share their food, even if it means they don't get as much. Dogs can feel when someone is sad, and they try to make them feel better. Prairie dogs even feel more connected to their partners after spending time together!

Guess what? Animals love to play! Ravens like to hang upside down and slide down slopes just for fun. Dolphins play games with seaweed, passing it to each other and making happy sounds. And chimpanzees laugh and have rowdy play dates. It's not just practice—it's about having fun and being silly, just like when we play!

Some animals even have special friends for life. Wolves stay with their partners forever, and penguins travel a long way to be with their mates. Lots of different animals, from eagles to swans, can be best friends with someone of the same sex.

They show love and tenderness, just like people do.

Sometimes, animals get surprised too! Dogs jump back when they're surprised, just like we do. Chimpanzees are shocked when they see fire or their own reflections. Even squirrels, cows, and monkeys play the classic shell game and act surprised when things disappear!

Animals can get mad too! Dogs growl, cats hiss, and bears roar when they're upset. Gorillas beat their chests to show they're strong. When animals feel threatened, they might get angry to protect themselves or their friends. It's like when we get upset when someone crosses our boundaries.

Animals also feel scared sometimes. Horses get scared of snakes, and monkeys have special calls for different dangers. Just like us, animals feel anxious in dangerous situations, and it helps them stay safe.

Even though we can't always know exactly what animals feel inside, lots of evidence shows that they have rich emotional lives. They feel joy, sadness, surprise, anger, and fear, just like us.

Charles Darwin, a smart scientist, said that animals and humans are not so different when it comes to feeling pleasure and pain. We should be kind to animals because they can feel happy, sad, and everything in between. Understanding their feelings helps us connect with our animal friends and treat them with love and care. We may be different, but we share a special bond with the animals on our planet!

Loyalty

Imagine a world where some animals, like wolves, are like best buddies forever. Wolf friends stick together, help each other hunt, and protect their homes. They even have special reunions every year at their favourite spots! These wolf friends are so loyal, and their friendship lasts until the end of their furry days.

Now, let's meet the bald eagle friends who are like superheroes of the sky. They do incredible tricks in the air, like flying and cartwheeling, to show how much they care about each other. These eagle friends always go back to the same cosy nests, and when they have baby eaglets, it's a sign that their friendship is super strong—they truly stay friends for a lifetime!

But wait, there are funny geese friends too! If one goose friend has to go to the big birdie playground in the sky, the other goose finds a new friend. They never break up with healthy friends just for fun. These geese friends believe in forever friendships, and that's really sweet!

Now, let's talk about squirrels and blue jays. They're like little adventurers looking for new friends, even if they already have a best buddy. And guess what? Red-winged blackbirds are kind of like having special territories with lots of friends, but they might have more than one special friend outside their territory!

Nature has a plan for every friend. Some animals, like barn owls and prairie voles, need both mom and dad to take care of their little ones. So, they stay friends forever, working together to raise their cute babies.

But, in other places, with lions and gorillas, it's a bit different. The lion boss has lots of lioness friends, and the gorilla boss has lots of gorilla lady friends. Everyone has their own way of making families work!

Sometimes, where animals live, decides if they stay best friends or not. If food and homes are spread out like puzzle pieces, animals like to team up and protect everything together. But if everything is close together, one animal can be in charge and share with everyone. It's like having a big family picnic!

Oh, and did you know that some animals, like gibbons and black vultures, really love spending their days with just one special friend? It helps them be super happy and take care of their little ones.

But guess what? Humans are special too! We have our own way of being friends, and it's not exactly like the animals. Our hearts feel love in different ways, and we make promises to stay friends forever. It's like having a secret code that only humans understand!

So, whether you're a wolf, an eagle, a goose, or a human, friendship is like a beautiful dance. Every friend has their own unique moves, and together they create a wonderful symphony of love and joy in the animal kingdom!

Animal Brains

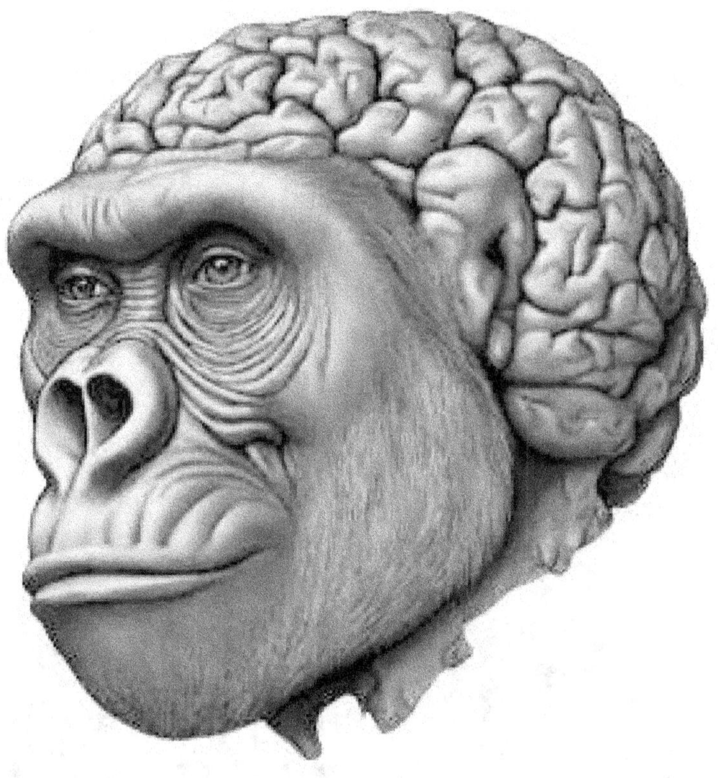

Did you know that animals have super cool brains? Yep! Each animal has a special brain that makes them unique, just like how you're different from your friends. Let's talk about some amazing things about animal brains!

Some animals, like elephants, dolphins, and apes, have really big brains, but humans have the biggest brains of all! Our brains are like supercomputers, filled with lots and lots of tiny parts called neurons and synapses. These help us do all sorts of amazing things, just like animals with big brains can do some pretty cool stuff too!

Inside our brains, we have parts that help us feel emotions like happiness and love. Guess what? Animals like dogs, chimps, elephants, and whales have similar parts in their brains too! Isn't that neat? Our brains are like big, complicated networks that help us think and learn new things.

Our brains are made up of special chemicals called neurotransmitters, just like animals' brains are. These chemicals help our brains work, even though we might look different from animals on the outside. When animals are babies, their brains grow really fast, just like ours do! Dogs, for example, can learn the names of over a thousand things, which shows how smart they are!

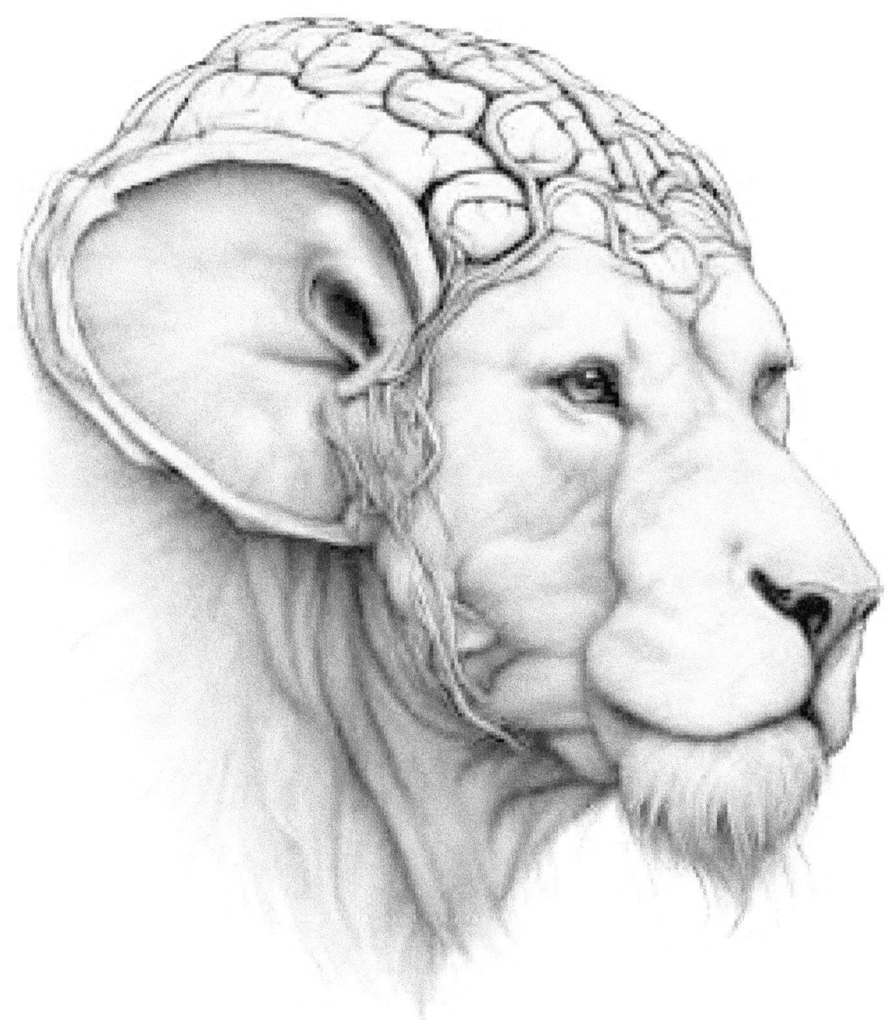

But, there are some differences too. Animals don't have a special part in their brains just for language like humans do. Instead, they use gestures and sounds to talk to each other. And while humans teach and learn from each other, animals don't do that in the same way.

Even though our brains might work a little differently, each one is special and brilliant in its own way. It's like how flowers bloom in different colours and shapes. We all come from the same big family tree, so we're similar in some ways and different in others. And all these differences make our world a super interesting and fun place to be!

How Animals Talk

In the wonderful world of nature, animals are like our special friends who talk to each other in their own cool ways to stay safe and happy. Just like when we share toys and talk to our friends, animals have super interesting ways of talking to each other too!

Monkeys and chimpanzees, who are like our cousins in the animal kingdom, make lots of different sounds and use their hands to say things. They have more than 20 special sounds they use to ask for food or tell their friends about danger. And guess what? Lemurs, with their big eyes and long tails, have funny "stink fights" to tell other lemurs, "This is my space!"

Under the sea, whales and dolphins sing sweet songs to each other. Whales sing big songs, and dolphins even have names they call each other with special whistles. And don't forget about the tiny insects like bees and ants! Bees do special dances to show where the yummy flowers are, while ants leave trails of smell to guide their friends to food.

Up in the sky, birds sing songs to say, "This is my home!" Wolves howl to gather their family together, and coyotes make quick yips to say, "This is my spot!" And elephants, with their long trunks, make deep rumbles to talk about their feelings and how old they are, but we can't hear it because it's too low for us.

Even though we humans love to talk and tell stories, animals were talking to each other long before us. They teach us important things and remind us to take care of our planet. Understanding their special ways of talking is like solving a cool puzzle that teaches us amazing things. So, let's always be kind to our animal friends and take care of the Earth, our home sweet home!

Problem Solvers

Let's explore how amazing animals are! They're like our friends in nature, and they're really smart and clever. When animals face problems, they use their brains to figure things out.

Think about monkeys, like orangutans, chimpanzees, and gorillas. Orangutans are like detectives looking for yummy fruits in the jungle. Chimpanzees use sticks to get bugs to eat and make tools out of leaves to drink water. Gorillas are super good learners and help each other, just like superheroes helping friends.

Elephants are big and wise. When it's dry, they share watering holes with their friends and have a big party. Wolves are like a big team, working together to catch big animals to eat.

Birds like crows are really smart, too! They make tools to find food, like little inventors. Parrots and ravens are like detectives, opening tricky boxes to find tasty treats.

Under the sea, octopuses are like builders. They use shells and rocks to make homes and keep their places nice and clean.

Even when animals have disagreements, they make up and get along. They hug and help each other feel better, just like friends.

We humans are smart, too. We can solve problems and make cool things, like computers and robots.

But the best part is, we can learn from animals! They teach us how to live together and take care of our planet. From big whales to tiny worms, animals show us how to be kind and take care of nature.

So, let's be friends with animals and work together to make the world a better place!

Devoted Hearts

In the big world around us, animals are like our friends. They have special ways of sticking together and being friends, just like we do!

Let's talk about wolves. Wolves are like a big family, and they love each other a lot. When one wolf goes away and comes back, the others are so happy to see them! They work together to find food and share it with everyone, just like when we share snacks with our friends. Wolves are very brave and protect each other, just like superheroes in a team.

Now, let's think about elephants. Elephants are like a big group of friends, and they really care about each other. When an elephant friend is not there anymore, the others stay with them and touch them gently with their trunks. Elephants remember their friends even when they are not with them anymore, just like when we remember our friends from a long time ago.

And what about geese? Geese are like best friends who stay together forever! They fly in a special V shape, and if one goose is hurt, their friend stays with them until they feel better. Geese are like friendship superheroes who never leave their friends behind.

Animals also have families, just like us. Eagles and wolves travel a long way to be with their family every year. Sea horses are funny because the dads have babies instead of moms! Animals take care of their little ones a lot, just like our moms and dads take care of us.

Here's something interesting. While animals are really good at being friends and family, sometimes people forget to be good friends. Animals try their best to help each other, but people don't always do that. We should learn from our animal friends and be good friends to everyone!

One more thing to know is that animals are loyal because they feel it inside. It's like having a special feeling that makes them want to be good friends. We, humans, can choose to be good friends even when it's hard. It's like being a hero by doing the right thing, just like our favourite characters in stories.

So, in the end, animals and humans share a special thing called loyalty. It's like a strong bond that helps us be kind and caring. Let's be loyal friends, just like animals are, and make the world a happy place for everyone!

Animal Moms

In the amazing animal world, just like human moms, animal moms take really good care of their babies! Let's explore how different animal moms are similar to our own moms.

First, when animal moms are going to have babies, it's like when a human mom is going to have a baby in her tummy. Elephants carry their babies for almost two years! That's longer than a whole year of bedtime stories! Dogs and cats get a little sick and feel different, just like human moms do. Some fish even carry their eggs in their mouths without eating until they hatch – that's a big commitment!

When it's time for the babies to be born, some animal moms face challenges too. Hyenas have a special way of giving birth, and zebras have to be careful because they lie down to have their babies. Whales and dolphins have special swimming patterns to help their babies come out. Despite these challenges, animal moms work really hard to bring new life into the world.

Once the babies are here, animal moms are super devoted! Cheetahs protect their cubs, orangutans teach their babies how to build nests, and polar bears lose weight while taking care of their little ones. Even seahorses let their mates carry eggs in a pouch on their bodies – that's teamwork!

When it's time for the babies to eat, animal moms give them milk. Elephants nurse for five years – that's a lot of snack time! Wolves and giant anteaters also have special milk for their babies. Even reptiles and fish have their own way of giving nutrients to their babies. It's like a special meal made with love.

As the babies grow up, animal moms teach them important things. Cheetah moms teach their cubs how to hunt, orca moms show their daughters where to find fish, and alligator moms carry their little ones in their mouths! Playtime is also important for animals – dogs play with their puppies, bears wrestle with their cubs, and cats bring toys for their kittens to practice hunting.

As the babies become teenagers, animal moms still stay close. Beluga whales form lifelong bonds, elephants lead their herds with wisdom, and baboon moms help their teenage daughters. Animal moms are always there to guide and support their children, just like our moms do!

Even though there are some differences between animal moms and human moms, like language and technology, the love and care they give to their babies are the same. Animal moms and human moms share a special connection in bringing up their little ones. As naturalist John Muir said, "Motherhood is a universal sisterhood." Animal moms truly are amazing!

Elephant Moms

In our big world, elephants are amazing animals. They really love their families a lot. When a baby elephant is born, its mom is like a superhero elephant, taking care of it and teaching it how to stand up. Then, the baby meets its elephant family, like aunts, sisters, and cousins. They all come together to say hello and gently touch the baby with their trunks, making it feel super welcome!

Elephant moms are great at looking after their babies. They give them yummy milk to help them grow big and strong. Even when the babies start eating plants, they still love cuddling with their moms for two whole years!

Elephant families work together like a team. The older elephants, like the wise grandmas, make sure everyone is safe and happy. They even help the young ones, giving the tired moms a break, and they show everyone where to find food and water.

Elephants have super good memories. They never forget their family and have special celebrations when they see each other again. They do happy dances, make loud noises, and sometimes even pee a little because they're so excited!

But elephants have some problems, too. Bad people might hurt them, and they might not have enough space to live. That's why it's really important for us to help them by giving them lots of room to be together with their families. This way, they can keep having their happy parties and the older elephants can teach the younger ones all the important stuff they need to know.

Elephants show us how much families matter and how we should take care of each other. They're like wise teachers, passing on important lessons to keep everyone safe and happy. We can learn a lot from these incredible animals!

Mommy Apes

In the big family of animals like us, apes are special because they take care of their little ones a lot, just like human moms and dads do! Let's learn about ape moms and their babies.

Chimpanzee moms are super dedicated. When it's time for a baby chimp to be born, the mom goes to a quiet place. After the baby is born, she introduces it to the group the next day. The mom makes a comfy bed of leaves, protects her baby, and feeds it whenever it's hungry. For three months, she carries the baby everywhere, only putting it down to eat or rest. If the baby cries, she hugs, rocks, or feeds it to make it feel better. This helps baby chimps stay safe and healthy.

As baby chimps grow, their moms let them explore and play. Even when the little chimps climb on their moms while eating or resting, the moms are patient. They teach the young ones how to find food and use tools, like playing games. If there's a disagreement, moms step in to help and make sure everyone gets along.

Orangutan moms are like superhero moms! They build a new nest high in the trees every night to keep their babies safe. Moms and babies share food and explore together every day. Orangutan moms even change how they move through the trees so their little ones can practice climbing without getting hurt. They take care of their babies until they are big kids!

Gorilla moms are also amazing. Baby gorillas are born helpless and need their moms a lot. Gorilla moms nurse their babies for a long time, up to age eight! Other gorillas help too - dads watch over the babies, and aunts often take them for playtime. As the gorillas grow up, they stay close to their moms and become important members of their big gorilla family.

Even though ape moms and human moms are a bit different, they share a special bond. Ape moms teach their kids important things, just like our moms do. We can learn from ape moms about taking care of each other and working together. By understanding and protecting apes, we also take care of our own big family in the animal kingdom. Let's celebrate and respect our ape friends!

Chimpanzee Families

In the jungle, where the trees are tall and the leaves rustle, chimpanzees are like our animal cousins. They are a bit like our family, and they teach us about how families take care of each other.

When baby chimpanzees are born, their moms take super good care of them. They lick them clean and make sure they are cosy in their furry arms.

The babies hold on tight to their moms when they go on adventures and only let go when it's snack time. If they get separated, the moms make loud sounds until they find each other, just like when we call for our friends.

As the baby chimpanzees grow, they learn to do things on their own, but they still need their moms a lot. Moms give them rides on their backs and stop everything to feed them whenever they're hungry. Being a mom chimp is hard work, but they do it with so much love.

Chimp kids learn by playing and watching their moms. They copy how their moms use tools to crack nuts or catch bugs. Moms let them pretend with their own play tools, and it makes the little chimps feel brave. Moms are patient teachers and always help their kids feel confident.

Chimp families also know how to be kind to each other. If there's a little argument, moms show everyone how to make up with hugs and kisses. They teach the chimp kids how to share and be friends. Chimp moms are like superhero teachers!

When chimp babies cry, their moms are there to comfort them. Chimp moms look at their babies with caring eyes and make funny faces to cheer them up. This helps the little chimps understand feelings and be happy together. Moms are like magic at making everything better.

Even when chimp kids grow up, they still spend lots of time with their moms. They travel and chat together, and when they're sick or hurt, they rely on their moms for help. Chimp families stick together, just like our families do.

Sometimes, the older siblings and aunts help take care of the little ones too. It's like a big family team, and they all work together. Chimp families know that it's important for everyone to help each other, just like in our communities.

But oh no, the jungle where chimpanzees live is in trouble. Trees are being cut down, and bad people are causing problems for the chimps. Their families are getting smaller, and they need our help to stay safe.

When we learn about chimp families, it helps us understand our own families. Even though we're not exactly the same, we all come from the same big family tree. Chimps teach us about love, kindness, and being together. Let's take care of our animal cousins and our Earth, so everyone can be happy and safe!

Animal Hunters

In the past, people were like our animal friends and they knew how to catch their own food. They didn't have supermarkets, so humans had to run and work together to catch their dinner. Even though we don't do that anymore, some things are still similar between us and our animal friends.

Nowadays, we don't hunt like we used to, but we still like to eat meat. Instead of hunting ourselves, some people help us get meat from animals that live on farms.

It's a bit like teamwork - just like how animals in groups, like wolves and wild cats, work together to catch their food.

Some animals, like big cats and bears, don't have a team. They like to catch their food alone, but they're really smart about it. Cats watch the other animals and pick the ones that are easier to catch. Bears know where the fish are and wait for them to swim by. It's like they have a plan, just like our ancestors did when they made tools to help them hunt.

But there's something special about us humans. We use tools and weapons in a way that animals don't. We made spears and bows to help us hunt better. We even created things that no other animals have - like machines and gadgets to make hunting easier.

One big difference between us and our animal friends is that animals hunt to eat, not for fun. We sometimes do things that hurt others just because we want to, and that's not nice. Animals don't do that. They only hunt to get food and survive.

Animals don't feel bad about hunting, but we do. When we hurt others, we sometimes feel guilty or sad. Animals don't have those feelings like we do. We also have a special way of thanking the animals we hunt. We respect them and say thanks for giving us food.

Even though we're different from animals, we can learn good things from them. Some people from different cultures thank the animals they hunt and make sure to do it in a nice way. It's like having a special rule to be kind to the animals that help us.

In the end, we're not exactly like our animal friends, but we can be good to them. We have the power to be kind and use our skills to help others instead of hurting them. We should be thankful for the animals that give us food and treat them with care. That's what makes us special and shows how we can use our abilities for good things.

Animal Magic

Creativity is like magic in the animal world! Animals do amazing things that show they have their own special imaginations. Let's explore some of the incredible ways animals are creative, just like we are!

Animal Artists:

Some animals are like painters and decorators. Bowerbirds make fancy homes out of twigs and decorate them with colourful treasures to impress their friends. Chimpanzees can even paint pictures! They use colours and shapes to express themselves, just like when we draw with crayons.

Music Makers:

Animals make beautiful music, too! Songbirds create melodies with rhythm and repetition, and humpback whales compose intricate songs that follow special rules. Wolves howl with fancy pitches and harmony. It's like they're having their own concerts in the wild!

Dancing Stars:

Guess what? Animals love to dance! Snowball the cockatoo dances to the beat, and some birds have their own special dance routines. Animals express themselves through dance, just like when we dance to our favourite music.

Clever Tool Users:

Some animals are super smart with tools! Crows make hooked tools to catch insects, sea otters use rocks to crack open shells, and chimps make "termite fishing poles" to get yummy food. It's like they have their own special tool kits!

Tricksters and Deceivers:

Animals can be tricky too! Racoons pretend to be hurt to distract others, and owls pretend to be in trouble to protect their nests. Monkeys even use tricks, just like when we play pretend games.

Building Masters:

Animals are excellent builders! Beavers make log dams and lodges with cosy rooms inside. Orangutans build tree nests with roofs and comfy mattresses. Army ants join together to create huge hanging nests. They plan and solve problems just like when we build with blocks.

Animal Creativity is Amazing:

While we humans are super creative in many ways, animals also have their own special talents. From building homes to making music, they show creativity in everything they do. Each animal has its own unique way of expressing itself, making our world a wonderful and creative place.

Sharing the Wonder:

Even though humans and animals are different, we both come from the same big family of living things. We all have a special spark of creativity that makes the world colourful and exciting. Together, we create a beautiful tapestry of life that shines with endless possibilities!

Gorillas

Gorillas are amazing! They are big and strong, but what's even more special is how they love and take care of their families.

In a gorilla family, there is a strong dad called a silverback, and he leads the group. But the heart of the family is the moms, aunts, and little babies. They all love each other, and this love keeps the family happy for a long, long time.

When baby gorillas are born, they stick close to their moms. The moms carry them on their tummy and cuddle them while eating or resting. As the babies grow, they become playful and climb trees. Moms watch them carefully and make sure they play nicely. Sometimes, if they get too rowdy, moms give a little warning or a gentle tap to keep them in line.

Gorilla families help each other too! If a mom needs help, aunts step in to babysit and take care of the little ones. They work together to raise the babies, and everyone in the family helps each other out.

As baby gorillas grow, moms slowly teach them how to be independent. Even when they are not babies anymore, the bond between moms and kids lasts a lifetime. Moms and daughters stay together forever, supporting each other and having fun.

Gorilla moms are like teachers too! They show the little ones how to make cosy nests for sleeping, find tasty food, and be good friends. They even comfort their babies when they cry, just like human moms do. This helps baby gorillas learn about feelings and caring for others.

The big dad gorilla, the silverback, is like a superhero. He protects the family by scaring away danger and making sure everyone has enough to eat. But, without the love and care of the moms, the gorilla family wouldn't be as strong.

Sadly, gorillas are facing problems like poaching and losing their homes. We need to help them and protect them, just like they protect each other. By learning about gorillas and caring for them, we can be like a big family, taking care of our animal friends.

So, let's be kind to gorillas and all the animals in the world. Together, we can make sure they have a safe and happy home, just like the gorilla families in the forest.

Animal Adventures

On our huge, awesome planet, animals have super cool adventures! They go far to find yummy food and cosy spots for their babies. Picture caribou walking in snowy places or butterflies zooming around like magic! These trips show us how amazing animals are!

Now, let's talk about some animal friends. Wildebeests are like travel experts in the Serengeti. They go on a special trip every year, walking over a million steps, following rains to find tasty grass for their little ones. It's like a big circle of munching and moving!

Birds are like flying explorers. Some birds, like pintails, fly from Alaska to Mexico, while others, like godwits, make a super long trip from Alaska to New Zealand. They travel to get the best food and enjoy sunny days in both sides of the world. Birds are like detectives following delicious clues in the sky!

Caribou in Alaska are smart travellers too. Pregnant caribou moms go to safe places by the ocean to have their babies. After that, they walk back to cooler areas, away from bugs that bite. They make sure their little ones are safe and happy.

Even butterflies have a cool journey! Monarchs fly a super long way, up to 3000 miles, to a warm place in Mexico. It's like a butterfly vacation where they can survive the cold winter. They're like little fairies floating in the sky!

Salmon, our underwater friends, swim against the current to go back to where they were born. It's a hard trip, but they do it to have babies. They're like superhero parents carrying important nutrients on their journey.

Sea turtles are like sailors of the ocean. They travel across big seas to reach their special beaches where they were born. It's like they have a secret map in their hearts guiding them home.

Whales, the giants of the ocean, go on mysterious trips too. Humpback whales swim a super long way from warm places to chilly feeding spots in the Arctic. Scientists are still figuring out why they do it – whales are like ocean puzzles!

Even little animals, like lemmings and gorillas, have smart moves. Lemmings dig tunnels under the snow to stay warm, and gorillas walk miles to find yummy food and cosy nests. They're like nature's architects building their perfect homes.

We humans are lucky because we can use special tools to watch our animal friends on their journeys. We have cool gadgets like tracking tags and satellites that show us where they go. But there are still some things we don't understand about their adventures – it's like they have magical secrets!

Even though we may not know everything, we can still appreciate the beauty of animal journeys. Animals teach us to respect nature and take care of our planet. We make rules to protect them, like promising to keep safe places for them to live. When animals move, the world turns, and we feel amazed by the magic of nature. Let's protect our animal friends and the incredible world they explore!

Under the sea

Deep under the sea, fish show us amazing ways of taking care of their little ones. From big sharks to tiny seahorses, ocean moms are busy keeping their babies safe and happy. Let's dive into the underwater world of fish families!

Sharks are like superhero moms. They have special powers to help their babies survive. Instead of laying fragile eggs, some shark moms give birth to live babies. Sharks moms, may keep their little ones safe inside for up to two years before they come out. Moms find cosy spots near the shore, where it's warm and full of yummy food, to have their babies. After they're born, moms stay close, protecting their pups until they're strong enough to swim away from danger.

Rays are cool moms too! They have a special way of giving milk to their babies before they are even born. Imagine having a snack before you're born – that's what ray babies get! It's like a secret underwater picnic. Seahorse dads are also unique. They help by carrying their babies in a special pouch until it's time for them to be born. This helps seahorse moms have more babies faster.

Some fish parents work together as a team. Daddy fish build nests and guard eggs, while mommy fish protect the hatched babies. Teamwork makes the dream work for fish families! Other fish, like damselfish and salmon, use their noses to know who their babies are. It's like having a special smell that only their babies have. Smart fish, right?

Fish moms may not talk like humans, but they have their own clever ways of taking care of their little ones. Mudskipper moms remember what their babies like to eat, and archerfish moms teach their young ones how to catch insects. Fish families may be different from ours, but they show us the power of love and teamwork.

Even though fish and humans have different ways of being parents, we all share a special connection. Just like fish families, we should take care of our world and the homes of these amazing underwater moms and babies. Let's be like superheroes for the fish and protect them from things like pollution and overfishing.

In the big story of life on Earth, parents, whether fish or human, play a super important role. We can learn a lot from fish families about love, teamwork, and taking care of our home. So, let's make sure to be kind to our underwater friends and keep the oceans clean and safe!

Talking Parrots

Meet the incredible parrots! These colourful birds are amazing because they can talk and copy the words we say. Just like us, they learn new sounds and words throughout their lives. Some parrots, like African greys and cockatoos, can even learn up to 1000 words!

Why can parrots talk so well? It's because they have a big brain compared to their body size. This special brain helps them control their voices and make all sorts of different sounds, just like us. They are super smart birds!

But parrots are not just good at copying words; they also understand what they say. For example, there was a clever African grey parrot named Alex who could name hundreds of things correctly. Parrots use their words to communicate with us and understand what's happening around them.

Did you know that parrots can combine words to make new phrases? It's like creating their own special sentences! This shows that parrots have a little bit of the magic that helps us talk with each other. Even though they don't speak exactly like us, they still give us clues about how language started long ago.

Young parrots are like little language learners. They quickly pick up on the words and sounds around them. But as they grow older, it becomes a bit trickier for them to learn new things. Just like us, they have sensitive times when it's easiest for them to learn.

Parrots are not just good at talking; they also understand things like shapes, colours, and sizes. It's like they have a dictionary in their minds! This helps them use the right words when they see new things.

Even though parrots are fantastic talkers, they don't fully understand the grammar rules like we do. They think of words more like patterns of sounds rather than a set of rules. So, while they can copy our speech, they don't use grammar in the same way we do.

Parrots may not speak exactly like humans, but they are still incredible birds! They show us a little bit about how language began, like the first threads in a beautiful tapestry. So, the next time you hear a parrot talk, remember that these clever birds are helping us unravel the mystery of language!

Understanding Dogs

Dogs are amazing friends! They're super good at understanding and talking with people. Dogs have been friends with humans for a really long time, and they've become really good at understanding what we say and how we feel.

Did you know that dogs are like little detectives? They can figure out what we want just by looking at us or listening to our words. Even better than some other animals! Dogs can follow where we point, understand when we want them to go outside, and even know when we're happy or sad.

Talking to dogs is fun too! They might not know as many words as we do, but they can understand a lot. Some dogs, like Chaser the border collie, can even learn the names of over a thousand things! They're like super learners.

Dogs are also really good at feeling our emotions. When we're happy and talk nicely, they get excited too! But if we sound a little upset, they know something's not right. Dogs are like furry friends who always want to be there for us.

Sometimes, dogs do special things to show they care. If we're feeling sad, they might come and give us a lick. And if someone needs help, dogs can go get help or comfort them. It's like having a fluffy superhero by our side!

Even though dogs are super smart, they do things a bit differently than us. They might not understand some tricky things or know about hidden secrets like we do. But that's okay because they're still the best friends ever!

So, dogs may not talk in the same way we do, but they understand us in their own special way. They've been with us for a long time, and they make our lives better every day. Dogs are like magical companions, making our journey through life extra special!

Healing Pets

"Being with animals makes us happy and healthy! Did you know that when you stroke a dog, it can make you feel better? It's true! Dogs are like furry friends that can help us relax and be happy.

Watching fish swim in a tank is also like magic! It can make people calm and happy, especially when they go to the dentist. Fish are like underwater friends that make us feel good inside.

Some people, like kids with special needs or older friends, really love spending time with therapy dogs. These dogs are extra special because they help us feel loved and not lonely. We can hug them, talk to them, and they are always there for us.

Having pets, like cats or dogs, is like having a special buddy. When we take care of them, they make us strong and healthy. And when we feel sad, they cheer us up with their love!

Even just looking at fish or birds can make us feel better. It's like having a tiny piece of nature with us. Animals are like superheroes who help us when we need a friend.

Remember, animals are our friends, and being with them is like having a magical adventure. They make our hearts happy, and they show us how to be kind and loving. So, let's be friends with animals and make the world a happy place together!

Dogs for The Elderly

When we get older, having animal friends can make us feel happy and healthy! Pets, like cute cats and friendly dogs, can be like magical helpers for grown-ups. They can make us less lonely and help us stay strong and happy.

Having a pet friend, like a fluffy cat or a playful dog, can make us feel better when we're feeling a little sad. If we stroke the cat or take the dog for a walk, it's like having a fun adventure! Pets make our homes lively and full of joy. They are like little rays of sunshine.

Walking with dogs is like doing exercise, and it helps our bodies stay strong and our hearts healthy. Dogs are great exercise buddies! Even if someone can't move around too much, having a pet can still be like having a special friend that makes us feel better.

Pets are not just fun; they can also keep us healthy! Playing with them and taking care of them can make our bodies strong. They can even help us live longer! Taking care of a pet, like feeding them or cleaning their homes, makes us feel proud and happy.

Pets are not just good for our bodies; they're good for our hearts too! They make us feel special and loved. Taking care of them is like having a secret mission. It gives us things to do every day, like making sure they have yummy food and clean places to sleep.

Pets are like our little teachers too! They can show us new things and keep our minds busy. If we teach them tricks or talk to them, it's like having a fun school at home. Pets are like friendly companions that make us laugh and learn every day.

Having a pet can also help us make new friends! When we take our pets to fun places, like parks or stores, we can meet other people who love animals too. It's like having a big family of friends who all love pets.

For grandmas and grandpas who have been together for a long time, taking care of a pet can be a special adventure. It's like having a new friend to love and take care of together. It makes their love even stronger!

But, before bringing a pet home, we need to think about it a lot. Taking care of a pet is a big job, like taking care of a little brother or sister. We need to make sure we have enough energy and money to keep them happy and healthy.

Sometimes, older friends might need a little help taking care of their pets. Family members can help with money or take care of the pet if the owner is not feeling well. It's important to plan ahead and make sure the pets and their owners can always be together.

Pets are amazing friends, but they can't replace our human friends. Still, having a pet friend is like having a little bundle of joy that makes our lives brighter and happier. Taking care of them is a special job that makes us feel needed and loved.

So, as we grow older, let's cherish our furry friends. They bring happiness, health, and a lot of love into our lives. Just like a shining lantern in the dark, they guide us with love and joy until the end of our journey, where love will wait for us forever.

Magic of Animals

Playing with animals can be like having magical friends who help us feel better and stronger! Horses, dogs, and dolphins are special animals that can make us happy and healthy.

Imagine hanging out with a horse. We can brush their soft fur, feed them yummy treats, and even go for a ride! Riding a horse helps us move our bodies and get strong. Walking next to a horse is like taking super cool steps to get better. Horses are so calm and friendly; they make us want to exercise and have fun!

Dogs are amazing friends too! We can pet them, play games, and do exercises together. When we hug or stroke a dog, it makes us feel relaxed and happy. Dogs are like superheroes – they can fetch things for us and open doors when we need help moving around. They love us and make us feel strong and brave!

Now, let's talk about dolphins, the ocean's clever buddies! Swimming with dolphins is like having a water adventure. They help us move our arms and legs in the water, making us feel so good! When we touch dolphins, it's like a gentle massage that makes us feel happy inside. Dolphins are great at encouraging us to join in and be part of the fun physiotherapy!

Sometimes, we have visitors like cute cats and dogs. When we stroke their furry coats or get little licks, it's like getting a big hug! These visits help us feel cheerful and excited. We can talk, move, and play with these furry friends, making therapy time feel like a party!

And guess what? When we take care of animals, like feeding fish or helping bathe dogs, it makes us strong too! It's like having a job that makes us feel proud and independent. Animals teach us how to be strong and heal ourselves.

But, we need to be careful too. We make sure everything is clean, and we follow the rules to keep everyone safe. When we do things the right way, having animal friends can make getting better even more special!

Animals are like superheroes on our healing journey. They help us feel less scared, more confident, and super happy. We walk together with them, step by step, until we can stand tall and strong all on our own. Our animal friends cheer for us every step of the way!

Other books by Author

Magical Tales

Share Your Experience

Dear Esteemed Reader,

I am thrilled to extend my deepest gratitude to you for selecting my book from the vast array of options available. Your decision to embark on this literary journey fills my heart with profound appreciation and excitement.

As you immerse yourself in the pages of this book, I hope you find yourself transported into the world I've crafted, drawn to the characters, and engaged by the unfolding narrative. Your experience as a reader is invaluable, and I would be honoured if you could spare a moment to share your thoughts.

Reviews serve as the lifeblood of any writer's career. They offer not only invaluable feedback but also guide other readers in discovering this book amidst the multitude of options available. Whether you choose to share a brief sentiment or provide a detailed analysis, your honest opinion holds immeasurable significance.

If the book resonates with you, I kindly invite you to consider leaving a review on the platform where you acquired or encountered this book. Your support in spreading the word would be immensely appreciated.

Conversely, if the book did not meet your expectations, I welcome your constructive criticism. Such feedback enables me to evolve and improve as a writer, ensuring that future works better align with the desires of my readers.

Once again, I extend my sincerest gratitude for your time, attention, and willingness to embark on this literary voyage with me. Your support fuels my passion for storytelling, and I am deeply grateful for each reader who joins me on this adventure.

Warm regards,

Scribble Sprout

Author of: Animal Adventures